so long, SHEA

Gary Carter leads his teammates onto the field at
Shea for a celebration after the Mets clinched the
World Series title in Game 7 against the Boston
Red Sox in October 1986.

Five Decades of Stadium Memories

TRIUMPH
BOOKS

St. Louis' Ken Boyer returns to a dugout of happy teammates after his fourth-inning home run put the National League in front 2–1 in the 1964 All-Star game. The midsummer classic was one of the signature events of the early days at Shea.

Triumph Books and colophon are registered
trademarks of Random House, Inc.

This book is available in quantity at special discounts for your group
or organization. For further information, contact:

Triumph Books
542 South Dearborn Street
Suite 750
Chicago, Illinois 60605
(312) 939-3330
Fax (312) 663-3557

Printed in United States of America
ISBN: 978-1-60078-243-5

Photos courtesy of Associated Press except where otherwise noted

Content packaged by Mojo Media, Inc.
Joe Funk: Editor
Jason Hinman: Creative Director

Nolan Ryan brings the heat against Hank Aaron in a May 1968 game with the Atlanta Braves.

Getty Images

contents

foreword

Prior to the 1962 MLB season, while at a golf tournament in California, I got a call from George Weiss, the former GM of the Yankees who was now running the expansion New York Mets. He asked me if I'd be interested in broadcasting Mets games on both radio and television with Lindsey Nelson and Bob Murphy.

As luck would have it, Lindsey was also on the team of broadcasters for the tournament. I had met him previously and liked him, so I sought his advice on whether to accept the Weiss offer. He told me, "Take the job." He confirmed what I already knew, which was that New York was a great place to be a broadcaster. But he really swayed me when he pointed out that because the Mets were a new team, we wouldn't be replacing any broadcasters for whom the fans felt attachment.

I told Weiss I would come to New York, and was soon hired. Lindsey, Bob, and I took pride in that we were going to be the broadcasters for the team that was bringing National League baseball back to New York. When the Dodgers and Giants left for the West Coast after the 1957 season, they ripped out much of the fabric and soul of the city. The Mets unabashedly borrowed their colors from the departed teams—blue from the Dodgers and orange from the Giants—and tried to revive the fanaticism.

The Mets opened 1962 with a loss on April 11 and didn't win until their 10th game. At one point, manager Casey Stengel, the team's biggest draw, admitted he worried his new team would finish the season at 0–162. As it turned out, they would finish 40–120–1, but their poor play (despite great effort) was what made them so endearing to fans, especially to those bitter towards the two best teams in the National League—the now-hated San Francisco Giants and Los Angeles Dodgers.

But the team improved, and paved the way for some monumental memories in the next five decades.

One year after the scrappy Mets moved into shiny new Shea Stadium in 1964, a young left-hander named Tug McGraw bested Sandy Koufax, claiming the Mets' first victory over baseball's best pitcher. Another thrill came two days later, when the Phillies' Jim Bunning threw the NL's first perfect game.

All of the twists and turns at Shea in that rocky first decade culminated in the New York Mets' 1969 championship season, the greatest year of all. Before '69, the Mets had never finished better than ninth place in the 10-team National League, but suddenly they exploded. Tom Seaver was the driving force on the team, always pushing the team to be better than they thought they were, and he led by example, becoming the National League's Cy Young winner with a 25–7 record.

The 1973 pennant-winning team, managed by

Yogi Berra, was memorable as McGraw's "Ya gotta believe!" became the team's rallying cry.

When Gary Carter debuted for the Mets in 1985 after being acquired from Montreal in the off-season, he won the opening game with a home run in the 10th inning against the St. Louis Cardinals, foreshadowing the coming excitement of the 1986 team and its cast of colorful characters. Despite the underachieving Darryl Strawberry, there was still a solid mix of young and veteran players like Carter, George Foster, Dwight Gooden, Keith Hernandez, Lenny Dykstra, Ron Darling, Ray Knight, and Mookie Wilson to carry the team to a world championship.

Ralph Kiner calls the action during a game against the Pittsburgh Pirates in August 1975.

The 2000 team, despite losing the Subway Series to the Yankees in five games, only fueled the feud between the crosstown rivals.

And since then the Mets, with bright young stars like David Wright playing baseball the way it's supposed to be played, have become competitive again. As the team bids farewell to the ballpark they were born in, they look forward to making memories for a new generation of New Yorkers.

Of course, there were also many memorable moments at Shea that didn't involve the Mets: the birth and growth of the New York Jets from their memorable run with Broadway Joe Namath to the New York Sack Exchange; a historic Beatles concert along with a number of other rock-and-roll acts; some major prizefights; and even a visit by Pope John Paul II.

As we look towards the future, may this picture book serve as a time capsule for not only the Mets and almost all of their first 46 years of existence, but for all the good, bad, and ugly memories that took place at William A. Shea Municipal Stadium.

It will be missed, but always remembered.

—**Ralph Kiner**

remembering

Shea

Amazin'!
The Mets run onto the field at Shea after clinching the 1969 World Series.

Getty Images

Amazin'!

It was the dream of William Shea to bring baseball to the site next to the 1964 World's Fair. With New York's National League teams exiled to California and the prospect of expansion unlikely, Shea was willing to create his own league to have a team back in the Big Apple. The conceptual Continental League would have its signature franchise in New York, and with baseball visionary Branch Rickey at the helm, the new league seemed to pose a threat to the established Major Leagues.

Of course, the Continental League never got off the ground, but one of the concessions the major leagues made was to add an expansion National League team to New York. Owned by former Giants minority owner Joan Payson, the new team was to be called the Mets.

The site of the new ballpark in Flushing Meadows was primed for a stadium, but construction took time. The Mets bided their time at the legendary but crumbling Polo Grounds for two seasons as the new stadium was readied for the start of the 1964 season. Dubbed Shea Stadium for the man that brought the National League back to New York, it was a glittering home for baseball's worst team.

The Mets were joined at Shea by another upstart team that they shared the Polo Grounds with. Led by coach Weeb Ewbank and colorful quarterback Joe Namath, the American Football League's Jets provided the first sporting highlights at the new stadium (to say nothing of a historic Beatles appearance in 1965). With "Broadway Joe" at the helm, the Jets stormed through the 1968 AFL season, toppling the vaunted Oakland Raiders to take the AFL title. Heavy underdogs against the Baltimore Colts in 1969's Super Bowl III, the Jets managed to shock football fans by winning the game and giving the AFL their first Super Bowl win.

With the winning example set by the Jets in the colder months of 1968, the Mets followed in kind during 1969. Formerly the laughingstock of the big leagues, the Mets had finally built their franchise around a dynamite young pitching staff, though they trailed a strong Chicago Cubs team for much of the summer. But after a black cat made a mysterious appearance at a game between the two teams at Shea in August, a Cubs collapse soon followed, and the Amazin' Mets were on their way to the playoffs.

After a sweep of the Atlanta Braves in the NLCS, the Mets took on a powerhouse Baltimore Orioles team in the World Series. The Orioles started quickly, winning Game 1. The Mets came roaring back behind strong pitching and did not lose again, taking the next four games to win a miracle World Series. With Jerry Koosman getting his second win of the Series at home in Game 5, Mets fans had something to cheer about after just eight seasons and found themselves at the top of the baseball world.

The cars of workers sit outside Shea's superstructure in March 1963. Though the stadium was originally scheduled for completion by this time, it's easy to see that the stadium is far from being complete.

Work had visibly progressed in the last month, but the stadium is still far from complete in this shot from April 1963. The open-ended design was intentional, and though the designers of the stadium had an option to completely enclose the stadium at a later date, it was never part of the original construction plan.

With construction just under way in July of 1962, the footprint of Shea is easy to see from the air. Though scheduled for completion by the first pitch of the 1963 season, the new stadium did not open until 1964.

opening day

(above) William Shea, the stadium's namesake, throws out the first pitch on Opening Day. Shea was instrumental in bringing National League baseball back to New York.

(left) The Mets and the Pittsburgh Pirates line the base paths on Opening Day. Fans packed Shea to see the new and glorious home of the Mets, while the Polo Grounds across town was being slowly torn down. In front of 50,312 fans, the Mets, as they so often did in the early years, lost — by a count of 4–3.

(opposite) The cover of a program from the Mets inaugural season at Shea.

1960s

The lights go on at Shea for the first time on May 6, 1964, with the Mets facing off against the Cincinnati Reds. Considered the most advanced lighting system in the world when it was built, the system's power was estimated at 2 million watts.

casey stengel

(above) Manager Casey Stengel hams it up with international fans of the Mets while introducing them to an American ballpark staple, the hot dog, prior to a 1964 game at Shea.

(left) Stengel waves goodbye to the Polo Grounds with his wife Edna after the final game at the old park.

1960s

(above) Willie Mays, left, winning pitcher Juan Marichal, center, and Johnny Callison, right, gather to celebrate in the dressing room after Callison's walk-off home run.

(right) Philadelphia's Johnny Callison is mobbed by happy National League teammates after crossing the plate following his game-winning, walk-off three-run homer that gave the National League a 7–4 win over the American League in the 1964 All-Star game.

1960s

1964

all-star game

dimaggio

(above) Yankees legend Joe DiMaggio signs autographs for fans at Shea in 1964. Though already retired for several years, DiMaggio remained an A-list star whenever he returned to New York. Although the young fans were not necessarily fans of the Yankees, they could not help but respect and admire DiMaggio.

(left) Former Mets manager Casey Stengel and Joe DiMaggio tip their hats to the crowd at an old-timers game held at Shea in 1970. The game was a testimonial for Stengel's upcoming 80th birthday, with Stengel serving as manager at Shea one last time.

1960s

(above) Workers ready Shea for a football game in September 1964. The American Football League's New York Jets moved with the Mets to Shea from the Polo Grounds, and college football games were played at the new stadium as well. Using movable seats, the new stadium was well-suited for football and it became a precursor of the mutipurpose stadiums that sprung up across the country for the next 15 years.

(right) Syracuse's Floyd Little poses with his mom following the Orangemen's 51–13 stomping of Pitt in 1965. Little had a banner day at Shea Stadium, romping for four touchdowns, including a 95-yarder.

boxing

Challenger Wayne Thornton cannot dodge the left hand of light heavyweight champion Jose Torres in their title bout on May 21, 1966. Torres was able to successfully defend his title, winning by unanimous decision.

SID BERNSTEIN PRESENTS
The "BEATLES"
Sunday
Aug. 15, 1965
SHEA STADIUM

the beatles

Considered one of the most important concerts in rock and roll history because of its outdoor stadium setting and huge seating capacity, The Beatles opened their 1965 North American tour at Shea during the height of Bealtemania. More than 55,000 fans packed the arena to watch, scream, shriek, and even faint, as the rock legends played their way through a 12-song set.

perfect game

Philadelphia right-hander Jim Bunning strikes out pinch-hitter John Stephenson for the final out of his perfect game on June 21, 1964. It was Bunning's second career no-hitter and the first perfect game in the National League in 84 years.

(above) A view of how Shea was set up for Jets football during the 1969 season. It is clear to see how Shea was designed to use large tracts of movable seating, though the end zones have dramatically different numbers of seats. Despite its flaws as a football venue, the Jets had a much better home than the crosstown Giants, who had to cram a football field into an awkward seating arrangement at Yankee Stadium.

(right) Jets quarterback Joe Namath tosses a pass over the outstretched arms of Oakland's Ben Davidson during the 1968 AFL Championship Game. Broadway Joe threw three touchdowns in the Jets' 27–23 win, setting up a historic matchup with the Baltimore Colts in Super Bowl III, the first won by an AFL team.

1960s the

new york jets

the 1969 mets

Getty Images

(above) With two outs in the seventh inning of Game 3 of the 1969 World Series, the Baltimore Orioles loaded the bases for Paul Blair. Blair made rock-solid contact, and the ball looked to be heading for the gap and extra bases for the Orioles. Though the Mets led 4–0 at that point, the ball dropping could have brought them back in the game. Tommie Agee, however, saved the day, making this sliding catch to rob Blair and end the inning. Agee had led off the first inning with a homer, and the spectacular catch was his second of the day: he had ended a Baltimore threat with his glove in the fourth inning as well. The Mets won 5–0 and never looked back.

(left) The scene on the field after Cleon Jones caught a fly ball to end the 1969 World Series. Jerry Koosman is being mobbed in the infield: he had just thrown a complete game to earn his second win of the World Series. The Mets had been underdogs all season but rose to the occasion, first in catching the Cubs in the National League East race, then sweeping the Atlanta Braves in the NLCS, and finally by winning four straight over the heavily favored Orioles in the World Series.

1960s

(above) Jerry Koosman leaps into the arms of catcher Jerry Grote after the final out of the World Series. Ed Charles is the first player to join the battery at the pitcher's mound to kick off the celebration.

(right) Tommie Agee connects for a home run in the first inning of Game 3. The solo shot to lead off the bottom of the inning set the tone for the game. It was the start of a big day for Agee, both at the plate and in the field.

1960 1969

world series

remembering

Shea

70s

Believe!

Pitcher Tug McGraw takes advice from manager Yogi Berra as teammates Jerry Grote, John Milner, and Felix Millan listen in during an early 1970s game at Shea

(above) Tom Seaver waves his hat with one hand and holds his brand new contract in the other as he looks out from the Mets offices after signing in February 1970.

(right) Willie Mays take a sweet swing during a 1972 game at Shea.

Believe!

Great expectations saddled both the Mets and Jets in the 1970s. With the Jets now part of the National Football League, it seemed like more Super Bowls would follow. Sadly, however, the Jets began to mirror the fate of their superstar quarterback. Joe Namath was hobbled by injury for much of 1970 and 1971 and never again regained his form. Though he eventually was elected to the Hall of Fame, he was anything but Hall-worthy in the 1970s. The Jets managed just a pair of 7–7 seasons early in the decade and after a one-season stint with the Rams in 1977, Namath retired.

The Jets floundered for the rest of the decade, including three straight 3–11 seasons. They did not make the playoffs again until 1981.

The Mets, meanwhile, also struggled to maintain championship form. Though the pitching staff was outstanding, the Mets' position players often failed to provide offense, leading to generally mediocre results. After the sudden death of manager Gil Hodges, the Mets sputtered under new manager Yogi Berra.

In 1973, the Mets sat 10 games under .500 and were in last place by the end of August. Thanks to the infectious rallying cry of "Ya Gotta Believe" by Tug McGraw (and his screwball), the Mets managed to turn things around. Although they only finished 82–79, it was still enough to secure a division title for the Mets. With Berra exclaiming that "It ain't over 'til it's over," the Mets managed to knock off the heavily favored Cincinnati Reds in the NLCS. Though they lost the World Series in seven games, the season remains a high point in Mets history.

The death of owner Joan Payson in 1975 killed the Mets' momentum, however. With her family uninterested in running the baseball side of the operation, they turned things over to M. Donald Grant. Tight with money and unwilling to negotiate reasonably with players, Grant traded Tom Seaver and Dave Kingman on the same day in 1977, a decidedly unpopular move still remembered as "The Midnight Massacre."

In 1975, Shea saw its busiest sporting season ever. With the Mets and Jets already entrenched, the team had to make room for two new tenants. The Yankees were in for two seasons while Yankee Stadium was rebuilt, thus bringing the New York Football Giants with them. The Giants moved to their new stadium in 1976, but for one year, Shea was the only place in New York to see any of the four major outdoor teams.

With the Yankees playing in Shea for two seasons and slowly looking better and better, they managed to take some Mets fans with them when the newly renovated Yankee Stadium opened in 1976. As the Yankees cruised to championships, the Mets languished, with attendance dropping heavily.

The year 1979 brought a tenant of a different calling to Shea. The newly elected pope, John Paul II, made his first United States visit to New York and Shea Stadium that year. With torrential rains threatening to ruin the event, the Popemobile entered Shea and the rain immediately stopped. It was a fitting end to one of Shea's most up-and-down decades.

clemente

(above) Pittsburgh's Roberto Clemente limbers up in the clubhouse before the 1972 season opener at Shea. Clemente reached 3,000 career hits on the last day of the season against the Mets. His life was tragically cut short in an airplane crash in December 1972 while doing charity work for victims of a Nicaraguan earthquake.

(right) A great ballplayer and great humanitarian, Clemente was recognized during his lifetime for his character. Admired by all in baseball, he is seen here with his wife, Vera, accepting the keys to a new car during "Clemente Night" at Shea Stadium during the 1972 season.

the new york

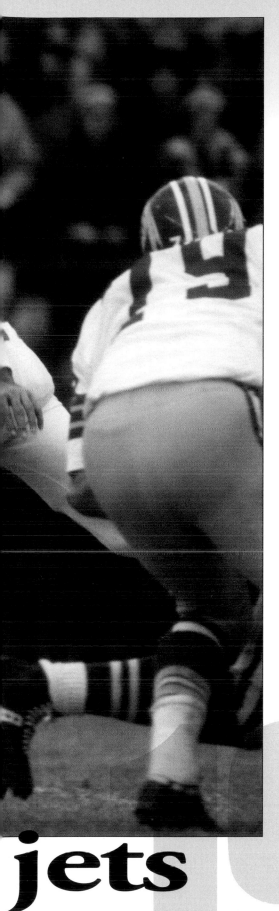

(above) A stylish Joe Namath looks on as the Jets fall to the Baltimore Colts 14–13 in 1971. Namath was sidelined with a separated shoulder, but the injury could not take away Broadway Joe's swagger or keep him out of his fur coat.

(left) John Riggins take a handoff from Namath and rumbles for yardage in a 1971 game against the Washington Redskins. "The Diesel" played for the Jets from 1971–1975 and rushed for 3,880 yards and 25 TDs.

jets 1970s

1973 world

(above) Willie Mays tips his cap to the Mets crowd during farewell ceremonies in September 1973. The former Giants great spent the last year-and-a-half of his storied career with the Mets, and though he was the oldest position player in the big leagues during his entire tenure with the Mets, he still put up decent numbers. He put a capstone on his career in Game 1 of the World Series, recording the first hit of the game for the Mets.

(left) The Mets' Wayne Garrett slugs a pitch off Oakland's Jim "Catfish" Hunter in Game 3 of the 1973 World Series. The first-inning homer gave the Mets the early lead, and they added another run on a wild pitch later in the frame. Hunter and the A's recovered, however, shutting out the Mets the rest of the way en route to a 3–2, 11-inning win. The win gave the A's a 2–1 lead in the series.

series 1970s

Tug McGraw winds and fires in Game 5 of the World Series. McGraw earned the save in relief of Jerry Koosman, but is better known for coining the Mets motto in their run to the World Series: "Ya Gotta Believe!"

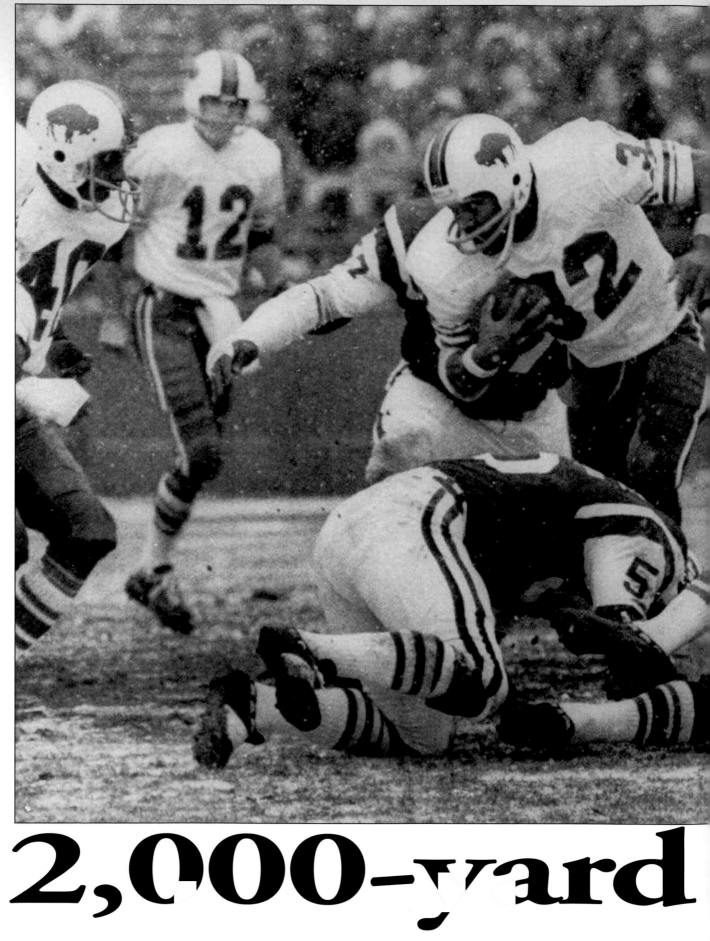

2,000-yard

(above) The Buffalo Bills' O.J. Simpson is carried off the field by his teammates after breaking the 2,000-yard plateau. The 2,000-yard season further solidified the Hall of Fame career Simpson was putting together. Though now remembered for his life outside of football, Simpson could do no wrong on the playing field.

(left) Simpson breaks through the Jets line on a first-quarter carry during a game on December 16, 1973. Simpson scored 12 touchdowns in 1973, but is best remembered for hitting the 2,000 yard mark in rushing, something that had never been done before. Simpson finished the year with 2,003-yards.

season 1970s

Tom Seaver holds his 1973 Cy Young Award early in 1974. Seaver had gone 19–10 the previous year, with a career-high 18 complete games. Though he won the Cy Young in 1969 and 1975 as well, Seaver has always maintained that his 20 wins in 1971 made up his best career year. Seaver is pictured here with Joseph Durso, chairman of the New York Baseball Writers Association.

seaver

Seaver delivers to the plate during a 3–1 win over the Houston Astros. After a disastrous trade sent him to Cincinnati in 1977, Seaver returned to New York in 1983. He was nearing 300 wins and would accomplish the feat in New York, only it was as a member of the Chicago White Sox, who had claimed Seaver in a free agent compensation draft.

After more than seven hours of baseball, the scoreboard at New York's Shea Stadium tells the story of a 25-inning game between the Mets and the St. Louis Cardinals, which ended in the early morning of September 12, 1974.

Brooklyn-born Joe Torre jokes with Mets manager Yogi Berra and general manager Joe McDonald in January 1975. Torre played until he was named manager of the Mets in 1977, though he did spend 18 days as player-manager. He retired as a player when he realized he could not effectively manage and play at the same time.

(above) Pope John Paul II delivers his farewell address at Shea on October 3. The pope had held office for less than a year, but had already made visits to his native Poland and the United States, setting a trend that would continue throughout his years as pope. He returned to the United States several more times throughout his reign.

(right) Pope John Paul II gestures to the crowd at Shea upon his arrival at the stadium, October 3, 1979. Fans braved heavy rains to make it to the stadium, and the pontiff brought the sun out with him when he arrived.

1970s

the pope

remembering

Shea

Resurgence

The 1980s Mets were a combustible mix of personalities and talent that meshed for a memorable decade and a 1986 World Series win.

Resurgence

The 1980s saw the loss of one of Shea's tenants, the Jets. With the team stuck in a tough lease that forced long road trips and late starts for Jets home games, the Jets sought to renegotiate terms for a new contract, while the Mets wanted to maintain the status quo. The football team began exploring other options.

The Jets played their 1977 home opener at the Giants' new home in the Meadowlands Sports Complex, but played the rest of the next seven seasons back at Shea before finally making the move to the Meadowlands. Though the Jets have had to make do with playing in a building called Giants Stadium, the more favorable lease terms and hugely increased seating capacity kept the Jets from being tempted to move back to Shea since leaving after 1983. Meanwhile, the emergence of the New York Sack Exchange, led by Mark Gastineau, Joe Klecko, Marty Lyons, and Abdul Salaam reinvigorated the team and the fans.

With the doldrums of the late 1970s carrying over to the 1980s, it was hard to see that the Mets were slowly getting better. With M. Donald Grant now long gone, Frank Cashen's meticulous rebuilding process was starting to bear fruit. 1983 and 1984 saw two Mets earn National League Rookie of the Year honors, with twin sensations Darryl Strawberry and Dwight Gooden electrifying the team and lighting up the league. Slowly, the team was also beginning to recover its fan base, which had been decimated by Grant's mismanagement and the success of the Yankees.

The team made its mark as an up-and-coming contender with the midseason trade in 1983 for former National League MVP Keith Hernandez, who helped spark the team's return to respectability. In 1984, Davey Johnson arrived as manager, and 1985 brought future Hall of Fame catcher Gary Carter to the mix. The 1985 season was a gas as the Mets won 98 games, but fell short of the postseason when they failed to sweep the division-leading Cardinals late in the year.

The 1986 regular season was much less dramatic than the Mets' runs in 1969 and 1973. The team pulled away from the rest of the division early on, winning 20 of their first 24 en route to 108 wins. Despite featuring Cy Young winner Mike Scott and former Met Nolan Ryan, the Houston Astros failed to better the Mets in the National League Championship Series, dropping Game 6 in a marathon 16-inning contest.

The World Series, of course, was magical. The Mets trailed the Boston Red Sox three games to two and looked down and out against their American League foes in the tenth inning of Game 6 at Shea. Down to their last out, the team staged one of the most memorable comebacks in baseball history: three straight singles to cut the deficit to one. Bob Stanley's wild pitch tied the game when Kevin Mitchell scampered home.

Every sports fan knows what happened next: Mookie Wilson's ground-ball somehow squirted its way through Bill Buckner's legs, Ray Knight scored, and the Mets evened the Series. Two nights later, Ray Knight socked a go-ahead homer and the Mets won their second World Series.

Though trades and off-field issues plagued the Mets for the rest of the decade, the team recovered to make a run to the playoffs in 1988. They dropped the NLCS to a Cinderella L.A. Dodgers club and the decade ended with a whimper when the Chicago Cubs won the NL East in 1989.

(above) Jets defensive end Mark Gastineau closes in on a sack of Dan Marino during a November 1986 game.

(right) The New York Jets defensive line of the early 1980s, known as the New York Sack Exchange and led by Gastineau (far right), along with (left to right) Joe Klecko, Marty Lyons, and Abdul Salaam, poses on the floor of the New York Stock Exchange before the season in June 1982.

rock and roll

(above) Art Garfunkel and Paul Simon perform at Shea in August 1983. The concert was part of their world tour following their reunion at the famous Central Park concert in 1981 that attracted over 500,000 fans. This tour was the last time the two played together until 1990.

(left) Roger Daltrey of The Who appears on the video screen above the stage during a 1982 concert at Shea. The tour was the last for original band members Daltrey, Pete Townshend, and John Entwistle. (Kenney Jones had replaced the late Keith Moon on drums by this time.) The band broke up the following year.

1980s

Mets rookie pitcher Dwight Gooden was just 19 years old when he made his major-league debut in 1984, but he showed poise and power from the start. His 98 miles-per-hour fastball and sweeping, devastating curveball earned him a reputation normally reserved for pitchers with many more years of service. Gooden won 17 games his first season, earning him National League Rookie of the Year honors.

strawber

Getty Images

(above) Darryl Strawberry looks out alone from the Mets dugout.

(left) Named National League Rookie of the Year the year before Gooden broke onto the scene, Darryl Strawberry was one of the most colorful and star-crossed players to ever don a Mets uniform. Strawberry is seen here celebrating a grand slam with teammates Gary Carter (left) and Keith Hernandez on April 28, 1985. It took until the 18th inning for the Mets to scratch across their fifth run, finally topping the Pittsburgh Pirates 5–4.

ry 1980s

Mets catcher Gary Carter rounds the bases enthusiastically after his tenth inning walk-off home run in April 1985 to beat the Philadelphia Phillies. A star for both the Mets and Montreal Expos, Carter put together a career that eventually led to his induction in the Hall of Fame in 2003.

carter

Carter is shown grimacing after forcing out St. Louis' Terry Pendleton in 1987. Carter won three Gold Gloves behind the plate and won the Silver Slugger five times in his career. He was an 11-time All-Star, and was instrumental in the Mets run to the 1986 World Series.

World Series MVP Ray Knight watches his seventh inning home run sail off into the night during Game 7 of the 1986 World Series. The leadoff homer off Boston reliever Calvin Schiraldi gave the Mets their first lead of the night after trailing 3–0. The Mets never relinquished the lead.

The jubilant scene at home plate, as Gary Carter leaps into the arms of Jesse Orosco. The Mets had just won their first World Series since 1969 in the most dramatic of fashions, and the final two games of the 1986 World Series remain some of the most memorable in baseball history.

Keith Hernandez hits a first-inning home run against the St. Louis Cardinals in June 1987. Hernandez had a personal rivalry with the Cardinals, who traded the 1979 MVP to the Mets in 1983 partially because they felt he was a negative influence in the locker room. Hernandez always felt determined to prove his old team wrong.

Dwight Gooden's pickoff move to Hernandez is in time to nail Houston's Kevin Bass in 1986. Hernandez won 11 straight Gold Gloves during his career and made five All-Star teams, but has never had much support from Hall of Fame voters.

remembering

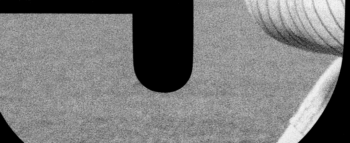

Shea

90s

Rebuilding

The 1990s saw the Mets try, try, and try again to get back to championship caliber, and ultimately they left the decade in better shape than they entered it.

Rebuilding

With the Mets the only tenant at Shea, the team remained competitive as the 1990s dawned. On paper the team was strong. Trades and free agency had brought in several big-name players, but personal issues had by now nearly destroyed the careers of Lenny Dykstra, Dwight Gooden, and Darryl Strawberry.

Still, the 1990 season was one of excitement for Mets fans. After a tough second-place finish in 1989 to the Cubs, the 1990 Mets found themselves in a divisional race with the Pittsburgh Pirates. Featuring young stars such as Barry Bonds, Bobby Bonilla, and Jay Bell to complement veterans like former Met Wally Backman, the Pirates managed to win the race with the Mets, reaching the playoffs for the first time since 1979.

The 1991 Mets managed to stay competitive, but the bottom fell out in the second half of the season, sending the Mets down in the standings. In an attempt to avoid the personal problems that had befallen the team in the late 1980s, management tried to reload again for 1992 by signing veteran players. It didn't work.

The Mets were mired in mediocrity as the experiment of building a team with free agents flopped miserably in New York. The high-dollar team had trouble with the press, with each other, and mostly, on the field. The team stumbled to 103 losses, the most by the team since 1965. Dubbed "the worst team money could buy," the Mets were in trouble again.

The year 1994 brought some clarity to the mess, as the Mets found themselves in third place. They had to do without star pitcher Dwight Gooden, whose career was disintegrating due to illegal drug use. Still, the Mets were in contention when a strike ended the season on August 12.

Over the next few years, the Mets slowly climbed back up the ladder in the National League. The team missed the playoffs by just four games in 1997. The next year, thanks to the addition of superstar catcher Mike Piazza, was even better: the Mets were strong again, but still missed the playoffs by one game.

Everything seemed to click in 1999. With the right players in place and a shocking sacking of the coaching staff at midseason to wake up the players, the Mets performed well all season, but still found themselves deadlocked with the Cincinnati Reds for the wild-card spot. Al Leiter pitched the game of his life in the one game playoff, five-hitting the Reds and sending the Mets back to the playoffs. The team won in the divisional round, knocking off the Arizona Diamondbacks in four games before falling to the division champion Atlanta Braves in the NLCS.

Two future managers collide: Pittsburgh's Lloyd McClendon is forced out at second base, but Willie Randolph cannot turn the double play on Barry Bonds in this action from 1992. McClendon later went on to manage the Pirates, while Randolph managed the Mets into 2008. Though he led the team to the NLCS in 2006, Randolph was sacked partway through the 2008 season.

Randolph is lifted from his final game in 1992. Best known for the 13 seasons he spent as a Yankee, the second baseman made six All-Star teams and was a six-time World Series champion as both a player and coach. He finished his career with the Mets in 1992 at the age of 37, and lifelong second baseman Jeff Kent made the start at shortstop on this day so Randolph could play his final major league game at second base.

Atlanta's Lonnie Smith lunges to make it back to first ahead of the pickoff throw to Mets first baseman Dave Magadan. Initially used as a backup with Howard Johnson at third and Keith Hernandez at first, Magadan proved to be an effective bench player and worked his way into the lineup with some regularity. He took over the first base spot from Hernandez in 1990.

(above) The Mets' Jeff Kent scores safely in the second inning of this 1993 game. Atlanta's Damon Berryhill has to leave his feet to catch the relay coming in from left field.

(right) Cincinnati's Barry Larkin slides safely into third under the tag of Mets third baseman Tim Bogar, successfully stealing the base in May 1993.

1990s

the

new york mets

Jeff Kent leaps for a wide throw in July 1995. Chicago's Brian McCrae is safe at second on his steal attempt, and Kent had to leave the game after injuring his shoulder making the catch.

(above) President Bill Clinton speaks during a tribute to Jackie Robinson at Shea Stadium on April 15, 1997. Rachel Robinson and baseball commissioner Bud Selig look on as Clinton honors the 50th anniversary of Robinson breaking baseball's color barrier with the Brooklyn Dodgers. All major league players wore a commemorative patch in 1997, and Robinson's number 42 was retired by baseball.

(right) Fans at Shea are treated to a fantastic fireworks show beyond the center field fence on the Fourth of July in 1997. Adding to the festivities was the game's result—a 6–2 Mets win over the Florida Marlins.

best infield

(above) Edgardo Alfonzo breaks his bat but knocks an RBI double in the process on April 28, 1999. Alfonzo was a key part of what *Sports Illustrated* called the "Best Infield Ever," playing alongside Rey Ordonez, Robin Ventura, and John Olerud. The tandem of Alfonzo and Ordonez was the most feared double-play combination in baseball in the late 1990s.

(left) Robin Ventura leaps to throw out Toronto's Shannon Stewart on June 7, 1999. A patient and smooth-swinging hitter, Ventura was perhaps the most complete third baseman of the 1990s. He is one of only five third basemen to hit at least 250 home runs and win five Gold Gloves, with a sixth added for good measure. Ventura made two All-Star appearances and attended the ceremony before the last game at Shea.

ever 1990s

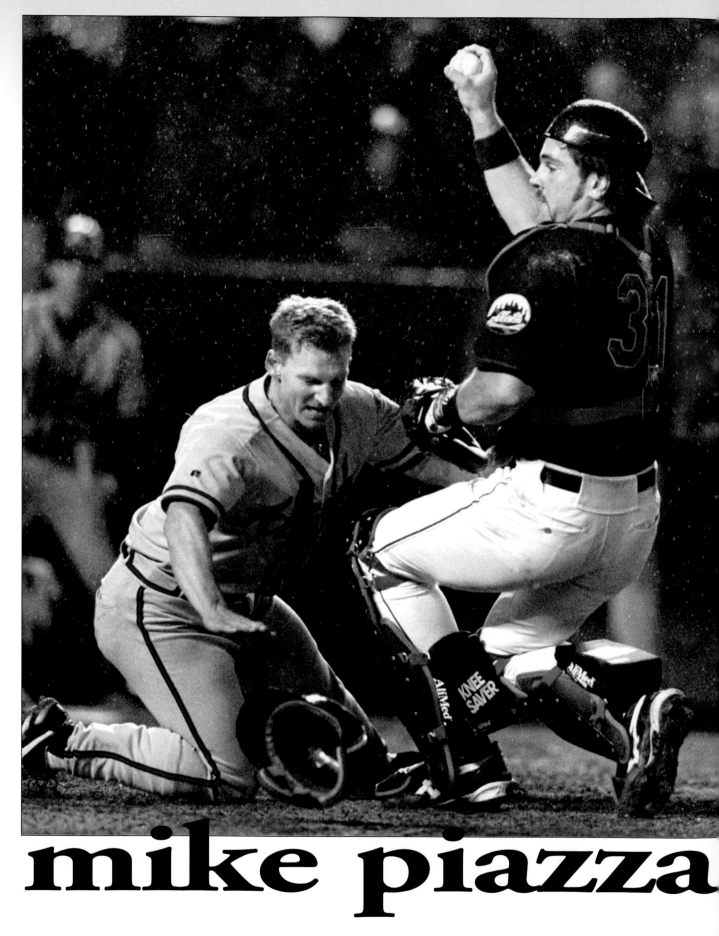

mike piazza

(above) Mike Piazza prepares to cross home plate after belting a walk-off home run on April 28, 1999. The Mets defeated San Diego 4-3. After his time in New York, Piazza spent time in San Diego before finishing his career with the Oakland A's. He finished his career as a 12-time All-Star selection and a 10-time Silver Slugger winner when he retired in May 2008.

(left) Mike Piazza tags out Keith Lockhart of the Atlanta Braves in the rain during Game 4 of the NLCS at Shea on October 17, 1999. The Mets defeated the Braves 4–3.

1990s

remembering

Shea

Competitive

Newfound aggression in the front office led to the addition of big-name talent on the field, and the Mets became a legitimate contender again in the 2000s.

Competitive

Expectations were high for the Mets as the new millennium arrived. The team had just been to the NLCS, and looked to be just as competitive in 2000. With the Atlanta Braves in control of the NL East (on a run of 11 straight division titles), the Mets set their eyes on the wild card and coasted to a playoff berth.

The Mets won their fourth National League pennant by beating the San Francisco Giants and St. Louis Cardinals, setting up a World Series showdown with the Yankees. The first all-New York World Series since the 1956 meeting of the Yankees and Brooklyn Dodgers, the Subway Series captured the imagination of New Yorkers.

Unfortunately for the Mets, however, they dropped the first two games at Yankee Stadium and faced an uphill climb back at Shea. Still, the Mets fought valiantly and took Game 3, winning the first World Series game at Shea since Game 7 of the 1986 Series. The win by the Mets snapped the Yankees 14-game unbeaten streak in the World Series, but it was the only win the team got, as the Yankees won the next two games and the Series.

Shea was used for a higher purpose the next year, as the heinous attacks of September 11th brutally damaged New York City—and indeed the entire country. With baseball on the back-burner for the first time in two decades, Shea turned into a staging area for rescue workers, serving as a field office and even as a place to sleep for some. The Mets returned more than a week later, temporarily reclaiming their home for a game with the Atlanta Braves, but Shea continued to be used throughout the post-attack relief effort.

Concerts filled the last decade of Shea's life as well, notably a three-night run by Bruce Springsteen and the E Street Band to close out their 2003 world tour. Billy Joel wrapped up Shea's run as a concert hall with a two-show performance in July 2008, closing the door on a venue that saw artists such as Prince, the Beatles, the Clash, and The Who grace its stage.

The Mets remained competitive throughout Shea's final years, even as Citi Field began to loom beyond the left field fence. The team reached the NLCS in 2006 and stayed in contention until the final week of the season the next two years. Finally, in 2008, it was time to say goodbye to Shea, as the Mets played one last game against the Florida Marlins, followed by a ceremony entitled "Shea Goodbye."

The Shea Goodbye ceremony ended in a fitting way, with Tom Seaver on the mound one last time. He hurled a final pitch to Mike Piazza as fireworks went off beyond the outfield fences, a fitting end to the stadium's historic run. While there will likely never be a spate of retro parks built in the style of Shea, and the multipurpose stadium remains a relic of the past, the fond, fun, and fantastic memories of the ballpark will never be forgotten.

(above) Jerry Seinfeld poses with Mike Piazza before a game in May 2005.

(opposite) Doc Gooden takes batting practice as a member of the Yankees before an interleague game against the Mets in July 2000. The game was the first appearance for Gooden on the Shea mound since the magical 1986 season. Though his career was beset with injuries and personal problems, Gooden rebounded and resurrected his career. The two teams were not quite finished with each other, either.

(above) The Mets celebrate their shutout over the St. Louis Cardinals in Game 5 of the NLCS on October 16, 2000, at Shea. The Mets won the game 7–0 to take the series 4–1.

(right) The Mets and Cardinals swarm the field after the Mets' Jay Payton was hit by a pitch thrown by Dave Veres in the eighth inning of Game 5 of the NLCS on October 16, 2000.

2000s

2000 playoffs

Fans cheer during the national anthem as players line the basepaths before Game 3 of the 2000 World Series. The Yankees had taken the first two games of the Subway Series, but the Mets jumped out in front in the second inning. The Yankees tied the game, then the Mets broke through with a pair of runs in the eighth to earn the win and halve their series deficit.

subway series

subway series

(above) Benny Agbayani walks off the field as Mets fans endure what they hoped to never see: the Yankees celebrating a World Series on their field. Luis Sojo had singled two runs home in the top of the ninth inning to break a 2–2 tie, and Mike Piazza — the tying run — flew out to give the Yankees the win. The Subway Series was bittersweet for Mets fans: It was a thrill to win the pennant and reach the Series, but the final result was hard to swallow.

(left) Jorge Posada slides to score the winning run in the top of the ninth inning of Game 5. Mike Piazza does not have the ball — it had ricocheted off Posada's back and into the dugout, allowing Scott Brosius to score as well.

2000s

after september

(above) The Mets' Rick White hugs Atlanta's Chipper Jones before the September 21, 2001 game at Shea. The Mets players are wearing hats honoring the emergency response units of New York City. The game was the first to be held in New York City after the tragic attacks on September 11.

(left) Firefighters cheer on singer Liza Minnelli as she belts out "New York, New York" at the game between the Mets and Braves on September 21, 2001.

11

2000s

(above) Billy Joel performs at the "Last Play at Shea" on July 16, 2008. Joel was the final artist to perform at Shea, and closed out a list of luminaries that included The Beatles, The Rolling Stones, The Who, The Police, Simon and Garfunkel, Elton John, Eric Clapton, The Clash, and Bruce Springsteen.

(right) Bruce Springsteen and Steven Van Zandt perform on October 1, 2003. Springsteen's *The Rising* was an album written in the aftermath of the September 11th attacks, and the album stirred many feelings in the Springsteen faithful. The shows in New York also brought controversy over the playing of Springsteen's song "American Skin (41 Shots)" because of its content involving a police shooting.

2000s

rock and roll

(above) The beloved Home Run Apple emerges out of the top hat and basks in all its red delicious glory after another Mets' home run at Shea. The hat is reportedly being moved to the Mets new home — where a new apple will be picked for the pop-out privilege.

(right) Because he shines on defense and when running the base paths, Jose Reyes has become one of the Mets cornerstones and has emerged as a fan favorite since his arrival as a rookie in 2003.

2000s the

new york mets

(above) Tom Glavine high-fives teammates after tossing a one-hitter on May 23, 2004, against the Colorado Rockies. Glavine is one of just 23 pitchers to hit the 300-win mark, sealing his Cooperstown resume. Though he returned to Atlanta in 2008, Glavine will be fondly remembered by fans in New York.

(right) Tom Glavine fires a pitch at Shea in May 2004. A five-time 20-game winner and two-time Cy Young winner, Glavine spent the bulk of his career in Atlanta, but had several productive seasons in New York. He signed a four-year deal to pitch with the Mets, and made his last two All-Star appearances as a member of the Mets.

2000s

tom glavine

(above) Carlos Beltran celebrates his walk-off two-run home run off former Mets pitcher Jason Isringhausen to give the Mets an 8–7 victory over the St. Louis Cardinals on August 22, 2006, at Shea.

(right) Beltran, left, celebrates with Carlos Delgado after Delgado hit a two-run home run in the third inning against the Washington Nationals on April 5, 2006.

2000s

beltran

and delgado

David Wright connects with his first major league hit on July 22, 2004. He had been called up the day before, and socked this double off the Montreal Expos' Zach Day. The 21-year-old Wright never looked back, and has been the Mets' starting third baseman ever since.

david wright

On the final Opening Day at Shea, fans look skyward to catch a glimpse of the fly-by following the national anthem. Cold April air ushered in the first series of the year — a battle with the division-rival Philadelphia Phillies.

the new york

(above) Small but mighty closer Billy Wagner delivers a pitch in the ninth inning of the Mets' 4–2 win over the Texas Rangers in the second game of a doubleheader at Shea on June 15, 2008.

(left) Mets manager Jerry Manuel argues with home plate umpire Bill Hohn after being ejected from the Mets' August 11, 2008, game. Manuel is in his second stint as a major league manager after leading the Chicago White Sox earlier in the decade. He replaced the fired Willie Randolph as the manager for the last stretch of Mets baseball at Shea, an exciting run for a playoff berth.

mets 2000s

(above) By 2008, Pedro Martinez was in his fourth season with the Mets and recorded 32 wins and 464 strikeouts.

(right) The arrival of Johan Santana in 2008 signaled to all that the Mets were serious about contending during their final Shea season.

2000s

power pitchers

A military C-130 transport performs a flyover — honoring families of soldiers serving in Afghanistan — before a Mets game against the Chicago Cubs on September 23, 2008. The Mets were battling the Cubs to stay alive in the playoff hunt, while the Cubs had already wrapped up the National League Central.

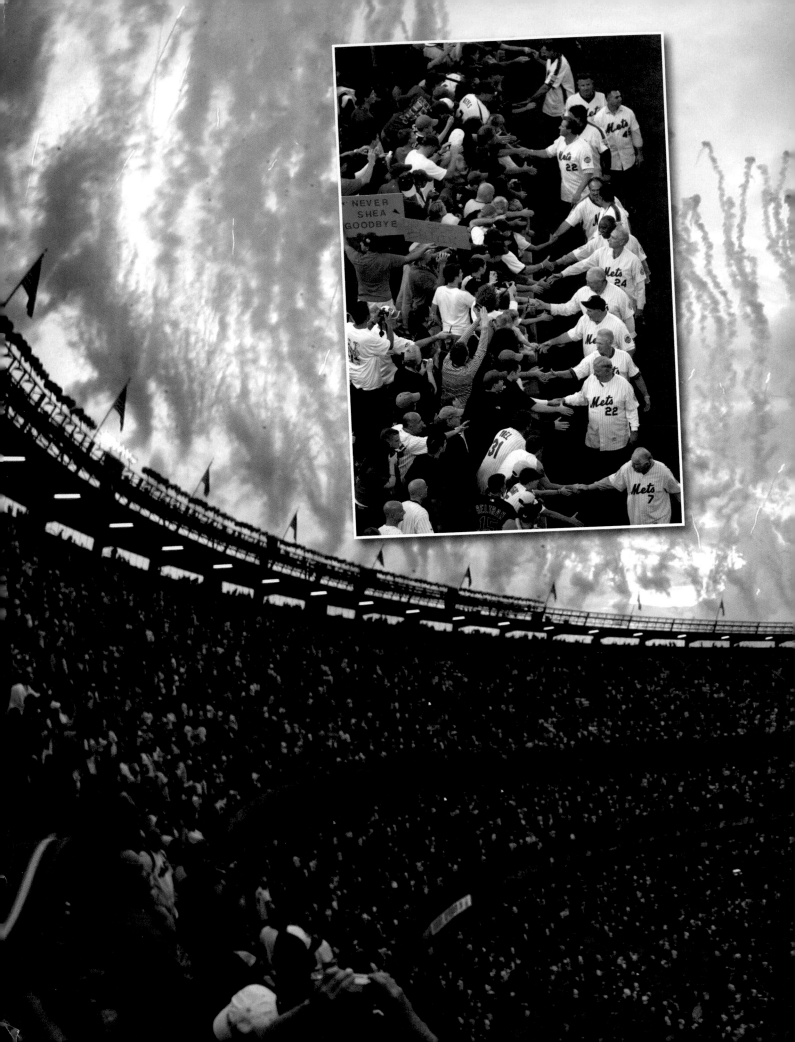

Fireworks fly after the last game at Shea. The Mets had fallen to the Marlins and missed the playoffs, but many former players were on hand to give a happy sendoff to Mets fans who packed Shea for the last 44 years.

Mets legends Mike Piazza and Tom Seaver turn
and salute the fans one last time as the Mets said
goodbye to Shea Stadium on September 28, 2008.